CLOTHES AND CRAFTS IN

ANCIENT
EGYPT

Richard Balkwill

Gareth Stevens Publishing
A WORLD ALMANAC EDUCATION GROUP COMPANY

Gareth Stevens Publishing would like to thank Lance R. Grahn, Ph.D., Associate Professor of History, Marquette University, Milwaukee, Wisconsin, for his kind and professional help with the information in this book.

For a free color catalog describing Gareth Stevens' list of high-quality books and multimedia programs, call 1-800-542-2595 (USA) or 1-800-461-9120 (Canada). Gareth Stevens Publishing's Fax: (414) 332-3567.

Library of Congress Cataloging-in-Publication Data available upon request from publisher. Fax: (414) 332-3567 for the attention of the Publishing Records Department.

ISBN 0-8368-2733-3

This edition first published in 2000 by
Gareth Stevens Publishing
A World Almanac Education Group Company
330 West Olive Street, Suite 100
Milwaukee, WI 53212 USA

Original © 1998 by Zoë Books Limited, Winchester, England.
Additional end matter © 2000 by Gareth Stevens, Inc.

Illustrations: Virginia Gray

Photographic acknowledgments

The publishers wish to acknowledge, with thanks, the following photographic sources:
Cover: C. M. Dixon/The Egyptian Museum, Cairo, top left and center /The Louvre Museum, Paris, top right, bottom left and right.

C. M. Dixon 5b, 9b, 14tl & r, 22b /The Egyptian Museum, Cairo, title page, 5c, 10b, 13r, 23b /The British Museum, London 3, 4b, 6t & bl, 7t & b, 9t, 11t, 12b, 13l, 14b, 16b, 17t & b, 19t & b, 20, 21tl, 22t, 23t, 25t & b /The Louvre Museum, Paris 5t, 6br, 8tr, 11b, 12t, 16t, 21b /The National Archaeological Museum, Florence 8l & br, 15b, 18t /Deutsches Museum, Munich 10t /The Egyptian Museum, Berlin 15t, 18b, 24t /Musée Borely, Marseille 21tr.

Printed in the United States of America

1 2 3 4 5 6 7 8 9 04 03 02 01 00

CONTENTS

Words that appear in the glossary are printed in
boldface type the first time they occur in the text.

INTRODUCTION

More than 5,000 years ago, the people of ancient Egypt lived in the valley of the Nile River, in North Africa. Every year the river flooded, making the soil beside it fertile. Crops grew well in this soil, and there was always plenty to eat and drink.

The Egyptians were skilled in **crafts** such as pottery, painting, and carving. They knew how to weave cloth for fine clothes and how to make precious stones into jewelry. The Egyptians built magnificent palaces and elaborate tombs for their rulers, the Pharaohs. Painters decorated the walls of these buildings with scenes of everyday life and pictures of gods and goddesses.

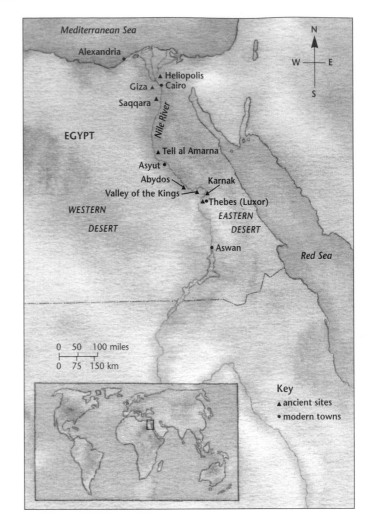

▶ Most of the land in Egypt is desert. You can see from the ancient sites and modern towns that people lived by the Nile River.

For more than 2,000 years, Egypt was ruled by kings and queens. Historians of Egypt, called Egyptologists, divided this time into three main periods.

c.2700 – c.2000 B.C. Old Kingdom
c.2000 – c.1500 B.C. Middle Kingdom
c.1500 – c.750 B.C. New Kingdom

◀ This drawing comes from a papyrus book, made around 1250 B.C. It shows a husband and wife wearing very fine clothes. They are standing in front of a table laden with offerings for the dead.

How do we know about the Egyptians?

People who study the things that other people made or built long ago are called **archaeologists**. They have found Egyptian paintings, carvings, writings, and many other objects.

Rich Egyptians lived in homes with carved wooden furniture and beautiful decorations made of clay, glass, and metals. They dressed in cool linen tunics and kept themselves clean and sweet-smelling. Men and women wore jewelry, for decoration and to protect themselves from evil. Poor people wore little clothing as they worked under the hot sun.

▲ A bronze figure of Imhotep, the architect of the pyramid of Saqqara

There were not many trees in Egypt, but reeds called **papyrus** grew beside the Nile River. People made ropes, mats, and even boats from papyrus, and a type of paper like **parchment**. Writers, or scribes, wrote on papyrus paper, and they have left us a full picture of life in ancient Egypt.

▼ The gold mask on the coffin of King Tutankhamen, who died about 1352 B.C. At this time, rulers were not buried in pyramids, but in tombs in the Valley of the Kings.

▼ Seti I ruled Egypt from 1318-1304 B.C. The inside of his temple is covered with carvings.

Things for the afterlife

The Egyptians believed that when people died, they went on a journey to the next life. They were buried with clothes, jewels, cooking pots, and food for the journey. The walls of rich people's tombs, the **pyramids**, were covered with paintings. The dry climate has **preserved** many of these items, so we know what people wore and what they made.

ANCIENT EGYPTIAN CRAFTS

Papyrus

In the marshes beside the Nile River, thick beds of papyrus reeds grew everywhere. Workers waded into the mud and shallow water to pull up the reeds. They tied up the reeds into bundles and brought them to workshops. Here workers would plait and twist the reeds to make ropes, sandals, matting, and boats.

Strips and layers of papyrus were soaked, pressed, and then dried. These strips were joined together with gum and made into rolls of paper. Papyrus rolls, or scrolls, were kept in boxes and jars so that the ink did not fade. Sometimes the writing was washed off, and the rolls were used again!

▲ A papyrus painting of a man and wife playing **senet**, a popular board game

How scribes worked

Scribes sat cross-legged with the papyrus roll resting on their knees. The writing material was stiff, so they did not need a flat surface such as a table to rest it on.

▼ A man hunts in the papyrus beds beside the Nile River.

▼ This stone figure, found at Saqqara, is of a seated scribe.

Wood

Trees did not grow easily in the heat of the Egyptian desert. Sycamore and tamarisk trees grew beside the Nile, and palm and fig trees were plentiful. Wood for boats and coffins came from other countries.

Most houses in Egypt had little furniture, but there were low wooden tables, beds, and even a kind of pillow to prop up people's heads. A carpenter used an ax and an **adz** to cut and shape wood. The blades of these tools were first made of flint. Later bronze and other hard metals were used.

Long planks of wood were very difficult to make. So joiners fastened small sections of wood together, one on top of the other, like tiles on a roof. Sometimes pieces were joined together by wooden pegs. This was skillfully done to make the sections of wood look like one piece.

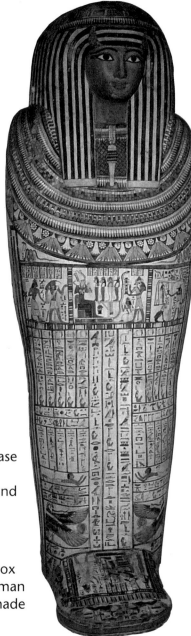

▶ This mummy case was made about 900 B.C. It was found at Thebes.

◀ This wooden box belonged to a woman musician. It was made in 1000 B.C.

The work of the woodcarver

Hard woods, such as ebony, were often **inlaid** with ivory. Carved wood was used to make **mummy** cases. The wood was hollowed out into the shape of the wrapped body, or mummy, which it would contain. Adults, children, and even cats and dogs were buried in these cases.

▶ A detail from a beautifully decorated glazed tile shows cattle grazing in the marshes.

Pottery

Potters used clay to make household objects such as storage jars for wine or water, bowls, flasks for oil, and huge pots for storing grain. Clay dolls and toys have been found, too.

There was plenty of clay in Egypt. The first potters took the clay or **silt** from places near the banks of the Nile River. They sometimes mixed it with sand to make it easier to work. The potters shaped the clay by **molding** it, or by building it up in thin coils. They smoothed the outside and decorated it with simple **geometric** patterns, or painted it red or black. The clay was baked hard in the hot sun.

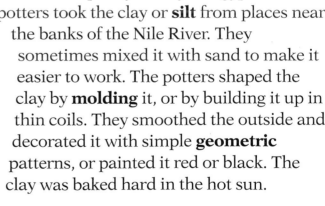

▲ This storage jar has been decorated with geometric patterns, using blue, red, and black paints.

▲ You can see vase painters at work on this carved relief from an Egyptian tomb. It was made around 1372-1354 B.C.

Later, during the Middle Kingdom, people began to use the types of potters' wheel and firing **kiln** that are still used today.

Bricks

The floodwaters of the Nile River left behind mud and silt. The bricks that were used to build houses and some of the pyramids and tombs were made of these materials.

Brickmakers mixed straw or sand with the mud and clay.

▼ Millions of bricks were used to help build this pyramid at Giza about 2500 B.C. Brick and earth ramps were made so that the huge stone blocks could be put into position more easily. The carved head of the sphinx is on the right.

They put the mixture into wooden molds and left it to dry in the hot sun. An outside coating of limestone was sometimes added to make the bricks stronger. Bricks were often decorated with a stamp to show the name or symbol of the pharaoh for whom they had been made.

◀ The lid of this pottery storage jar represents a god, Duamutef, who had the head of a jackal.

A bed of bricks

Mud bricks were used to make a bench outside houses. Young workers or guards could sleep on the bench as the nights were always dry.

Glass

Pliny was a Roman historian who lived many hundreds of years after the time of the ancient Egyptians. He wrote that some Egyptian merchants invented glass by accident. They lit a fire on a sandy beach. They rested their cooking pots on lumps of natron (a kind of soda). In the morning they noticed that some natron and sand had melted and made a shiny, hard material–glass.

Historians now say that this story is not quite correct. However, it is true that from the time of the Middle Kingdom onward, the Egyptians knew how to make glass.

▲ A glass jar made between 1500 and 200 B.C., before glass blowing was used in Egypt

Egyptian glass facts

- Glass was used to make small jars for perfume or ointment and for jewelry.
- Glass blowing was not known in Egypt until Roman times.
- Modern glass is heated to temperatures of about 2,700° F (1,482° C). Furnaces in Egypt could reach only 1,800° F (982° C), so the glass had little bubbles of air in it.

Glass makers heated sand and mixed it with lime and plant ash. They did not blow glass into shape. First they

▶ This pendant was found in the tomb of Tutankhamen. It depicts the vulture of Upper Egypt. The pendant is made of gold and decorated with **enamel**.

◀ You can see where the bright blue glaze, or faience, has worn off this figurine, which was made around 600 B.C. The sow and her piglets were sacred to the Egyptian sky goddess, Nut.

molded a mixture of clay and weeds or leaves onto a stick and shaped it like the inside of a jar. They dipped this into molten glass and wrapped coils of soft glass around it. They used copper and **cobalt** to color the glass green or blue. The outside of the glass was smoothed and decorated, and then the glass was baked in a furnace.

After the glass had cooled, the clay mixture inside it was broken up and removed through the neck of the jar.

Faience

Egyptian craft workers made objects to look like precious stones. The objects were

▲ A faience amulet of Bes, a god who protected people from evil

made from a thick paste of sand mixed with ash or lime with a bright blue glaze on the outside. This material is now called **faience**.

The oldest Egyptian faience objects were beads and necklaces. Later there were statues of animals, beautiful bowls, and jars. Some were decorated with birds and lotus leaves.

Lucky charms
- Tiny lucky charms are called **amulets**.
- The word *amulet* comes from the Arabic word meaning "protection from evil."
- Egyptian men and women wore amulets around their necks to keep them safe.

Metals

The most common metals found in ancient Egypt were copper, tin, and iron. Metalworkers, or smelters, also made bronze (a mixture of copper and tin). Hard metals were used to make sharp blades for tools or weapons. Softer metals, like lead, were used to make containers for water or to cover wood or stone to make it last longer.

▲ These gold and **lapis-lazuli** figures of the Egyptian gods Osiris, Horus, and Isis were made between 950 and 730 B.C.

Huge bronze statues and carvings have been found in tombs, but Egyptians also made smaller articles like cups, bowls, and jewelry out of copper and bronze.

A god with iron bones

Iron was not widely used in Egypt. Even in the dry climate, a red rust would form on the metal. Egyptians believed that this color showed the work of Set, the god of evil, whose bones were said to be made of iron.

◀ This bronze figure of a falcon, which was painted and inlaid with gold, was made around 590 B.C. He carries a solar disc and wears a neck decoration of the Egyptian sun god, Ra.

Gold and silver

Gold was very highly valued by the Egyptians. Its yellow color, like that of the sun, was thought to be the work of the gods. The wealthiest people wore gold jewelry. The finest and richest of treasures found in the tombs of the Pharaohs were made in solid gold, such as the famous portrait mask that covered Tutankhamen's head. It weighs about 22 pounds (10 kilograms).

A Greek historian called Diodorus describes a gold mining town in southern Egypt. Hundreds of workers lived in stone huts, each with a granite hand mill. They used the mills to crush **quartz**. The quartz dust was then washed, and tiny flecks of gold were collected for **smelting**. Work went on day and night. Workers were chained and beaten, and not allowed to

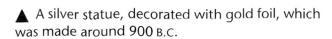

▲ A silver statue, decorated with gold foil, which was made around 900 B.C.

▲ The gold mask on the mummy case of Tutankhamen.

stop work even when they became ill. Over it all the sun burned down on this harsh desert place.

Silver, a softer metal, was not found in Egypt. It was imported and used to make jewelry. It was also mixed with gold to make electrum. This mixture was whiter or paler than gold in color and was used to make ornamental vases.

▲ The temple to Amon, one of the most important Egyptian gods, was started at Luxor by the ruler Amenhotep III. Work began around 1350 B.C. and was finished around 1213 B.C. The avenue leading from the temple is lined by stone carved sphinxes. The avenue was used for processions between Karnak and Luxor.

Stone

In ancient Egypt, before the Old Kingdom, people carved stone to make their tools and weapons. Flint was used for the tips of arrows and for the blades of knives and daggers.

◀ A sandstone sculpture of an Egyptian high priest, made around 1900 B.C.

▲ Huge carved pillars in the hall of the temple of Seti I, at Abydos, which was built around 1300 B.C.

Many of the pyramids in ancient Egypt are made from soft limestone, which was found everywhere. Harder stone, such as white limestone, granite, and **alabaster**, were dug out of special quarries.

Stonemasons made huge statues and **obelisks** from granite and alabaster. There are many famous paintings of these huge carvings. The paintings show how the figures were moved, either by boat or on rollers. One picture shows an alabaster statue 13 cubits (about 20 feet/6 meters) high, of prince Dhuthotep. About 172 men

◀ A stone relief of a horse's head made around 1300 B.C. It was found at Tell el-Amarna.

Pictures in stone

Many scenes of ancient Egypt were carved directly into the stone on the inside walls of tombs. The lines of the picture were cut in the rock or stone, leaving the image standing out in relief.

▼ A painted relief of Maat, the Egyptian goddess of truth, made around 1300 B.C.

are dragging the statue, harnessed by four long ropes, while overseers shout commands.

Precious stones

Egyptian men and women wore jewelry for decoration, as well as amulets to keep them safe. People wore collars and necklaces of gold, glass, and precious stones. Jewels such as amethyst, cornelian, and lapis lazuli were inlaid into metal frames or carved and fitted into rings. Women wore anklets and bracelets and sometimes a golden girdle around the waist. Earrings were also common.

Jewelry for the dead

Jewelry was placed on the dead to help them in their journey to the next life. Rich people had rings made of gold. Poor people had to make do with rings made of carved glass, or even straw. An ornament was placed over the heart, to protect it from evil spirits.

Painting

We know a great deal about life in ancient Egypt thanks to the artists who painted on the inside walls of tombs. The darkness and the dry climate have preserved these pictures well.

Egyptian painters often showed a complete story in one picture. They painted people from the side, not from the front.

The artist's palette

Egyptian painters had few colors to choose from. Red and yellow came from ocher, clay colored by iron, and sulfur. Blue came from azurite, and green from **malachite**. Soot and **gypsum** were used to make black paint. Brushes for painting large areas were made from bundles of palms. For finer work, painters chewed the end of a piece of wood to make bristles.

Scribes

Writers, or scribes, were very important because most people could not read or write. The job of writing was often

▲ A stone carving of the royal scribe and reader-in-chief, Nebmertouf

◄ A wall painting from a tomb at Thebes, made around 1400 B.C. It shows a horse, chariot, and an attendant.

Scribes did not write poetry or stories to entertain. They made a record of laws, agreements, and levels of taxes or of events in the homes of rich people.

Scribes used brushes and ink to write on papyrus. Papyrus reeds were used to make brushes. Ink was made by adding water to soot or **charcoal**, or to minerals that had been ground up.

▲ A papyrus painting made around 1340-1300 B.C., by a scribe called Hakhte

handed down from father to son. Girls were not taught to be scribes.

Ancient Egyptian writing is made of many tiny pictures, called **hieroglyphs**. The word comes from two Greek words meaning "sacred carvings." Pictures form each letter and often look like the object they stand for.

Which way around?

Ancient Egyptian hieroglyphs can be written starting from the left, starting from the right, or starting at the top and going down. How do you know where to start reading? Just look at which way the animals and people are facing–they always face toward the beginning of the line.

Counting in ancient Egypt

The Egyptian counting system was based on the number 10.
100 was shown by a coil of rope.
1,000 was a lotus flower.
10,000 showed a finger.
100,000 was represented by a tadpole.

▲ A list of offerings for a state official, which shows the hieroglyph for 100 (a coil of rope) very clearly.

CLOTHES AND JEWELRY

Grass, reeds, and a tough plant called hemp were also used to make cloth, but this was most often turned into matting. Historians disagree about the use of wool.

The most common material used to make clothing in Egypt was linen. Linen is made from a plant called **flax**. The young green plants were used to make fine thread. When the plant turned yellow, it was best for making linen cloth. When fully ripe, it was used to make mats and ropes. The finest material, worn by rich people, was called "royal linen."

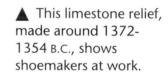 This limestone relief, made around 1372-1354 B.C., shows shoemakers at work.

Leather
Leather was widely used to make thick clothes or shoes. Vellum was a fine leather that was used to write on.

◀ A wall painting from the 14th century B.C. shows a man and woman dancing. Both are wearing fine linen clothes and decorated collars. You can see that the man is wearing sandals.

It seems likely that wool was used to make warm clothes, such as cloaks to wear in the desert when the nights were cold. Cotton and silk came into Egypt at the end of the New Kingdom, about 2,500 years ago.

Weaving and dyeing

The flax stems, or **fibers**, were first dried and then rolled to form threads. This process was called roving. Spindles were then used to spin the thread into balls. The threads were then placed on a **loom** and woven to form cloth. Men did most of the weaving jobs. The main task of women was to train and supervise the workers in the workshops.

People have used plants to make dyes for cloth for thousands of years. Blue came from plants called woad and indigo. Madder and **henna** produced red colors. Yellow came from the saffron crocus and could be mixed with indigo to make green.

▲ A detail from a papyrus painting, which shows a man wearing white linen clothes.

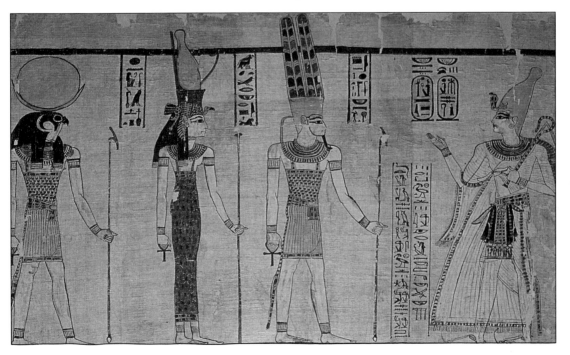

◀ Ramses III, who ruled Egypt from about 1182–1151 B.C., is on the right of the painting. He stands in front of three Egyptian gods. They all wear different styles of clothes and elaborate headdresses.

Clothes in life and death

The dry, dark conditions in ancient Egyptian tombs have helped to preserve some of the cloth inside, so we do know something about clothes and the materials used to make them.

Paintings and carvings can also provide clues to what people wore. But archaeologists have to be careful in drawing conclusions. People sometimes insisted that they were to be shown wearing their best clothes, or in clothes of an earlier time. People loved to look good and remember old times just as they do today!

Clothes for the dead

In the tombs of the wealthy, the bodies were sometimes dressed in their finest robes.

Other people were simply wrapped in strips of cloth, torn from old clothes. These words were said at the funeral of someone who lived in the New Kingdom: "She who was rich in fine linen, who loved clothes, lies in the castoff garments of yesterday."

▼ This papyrus painting shows a ceremony that took place just before the mummy was placed in the tomb. You can see strips of cloth on the mummy, which is held by Anubis, the Egyptian god of the dead.

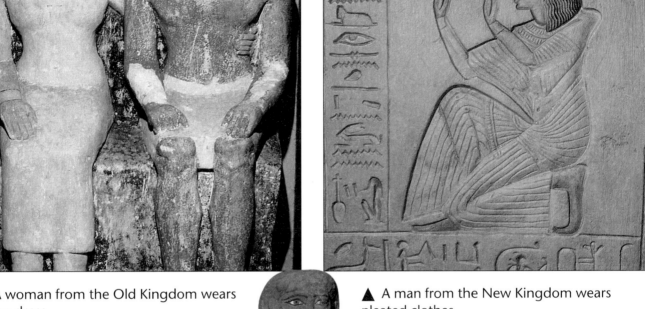

▲ A woman from the Old Kingdom wears a tube dress.

▲ A man from the New Kingdom wears pleated clothes.

Simple clothes for the heat

In the oldest times, women wore a simple tube dress. A piece of linen was sewn down one side, and straps added at the top held the dress over the shoulders. White was a symbol of purity, so the material was often left undyed. Later collars with colored patterns were added. In the New Kingdom there was much more decoration and bright color in clothes.

Men in the Old Kingdom wore a simple kilt. They wrapped a piece of cloth around the middle of the body and fastened it at the waist.

By the time of the Middle Kingdom, the kilt had become longer and straighter, while fringes and pleats were added later, in the time of the New Kingdom.

◀ This wooden figure shows a man wearing a simple kilt.

Pleats

Pleats, or folds, were made by pressing the fabric onto a wooden board with grooves in it. The pleats were kept in place by a type of starch.

Clothes for different occasions

Most children wore a simple **loincloth** or tunic dress. But in the palaces of the rich, children wore the same elegant uniforms and dresses as their parents.

Dress gave an idea of rank. A lord might wear a broad band of cloth over his cloak to show his authority. The overseer of workers might wear a narrow band or ribbon around his neck to show his position.

Egyptians loved to dress up for special occasions. Rich people wore beautiful clothes. Women and men wore long skirts or dresses fastened by clasps or brooches of precious metal. Sometimes they wore the patterned skin of an animal, such as a panther, over the shoulders.

▶ A wall painting from Thebes, made in the 12th century B.C., showing the Pharaoh Amenhotep I

Royal dress

Kings were often dressed as warriors. Queens sometimes wore long transparent dresses made from a very fine linen.

◀ This detail from a wall painting at Luxor shows a pharaoh and his son dressed for a special occasion.

▲ Queen Ahmose Nofretari (1575-1505 B.C.) may have outlived her son, Amenhotep I.

Sewing and mending

Needles and thimbles have survived. They were used for embroidering cloth, sewing decorations on clothes, and for mending.

Washing and mending clothes

Egyptians took pride in keeping their clothes clean. The jobs of Royal Chief Washer or Royal Chief Bleacher were very important. These jobs were done by men.

They washed the linen clothes on the banks of the Nile River. Many clothes were stained by the colored wax that people placed on their heads at feasts and that melted into their clothes. Dirty linen was rolled up into a ball, soaked in water, and then rubbed with a cleansing agent called natron. Clean linen was folded and locked in boxes.

Laundry clues

Scribes copied laundry lists, and some of these lists have survived. From them we can tell the kinds of clothes that rich people wore.

▼ An Egyptian sculpture of the wife of a prince was made around 2600-2500 B.C. The embroidered headband keeps her wig in place.

▲ Queen Nefertiti, who ruled Egypt when her husband died about 1335 B.C. The front of her crown carries the symbol of a rearing cobra, or *uraeus*, which was thought to protect the ruler.

Headdresses

- Some people wore headdresses to show their position or rank. Some were embroidered or decorated with gold or jewels.
- The pharaoh wore a crown on special occasions. At other times he wore a royal headcloth.
- Sometimes the pharaoh wore a red and white crown. White was the color for Upper Egypt, and red was the color for Lower Egypt.

▼ The lady Ray, wearing a wig held in place by a gold headband

Shoes

In the Old and Middle Kingdoms, most Egyptians walked barefoot. In later times men wore sandals made of papyrus or leather. They were forbidden to wear them inside houses or in the presence of someone superior to them.

Makeup

Men and women used makeup or cosmetics to give color and beauty to their appearance. A powder called kohl was used to darken the skin around the eyes. Rouge was used on the cheeks and lips. People used mirrors made of polished copper or bronze.

▲ A seated man is wearing a wig and a false beard. The painting is on a coffin lid made around 1050 B.C.

Hair and wigs

The Egyptians were very careful about keeping clean. Young children had their heads shaved bald. As they got older, children grew their hair. Rich boys and girls had their hair plaited by servants every day. Women wore their hair long.

On special occasions rich women also wore elaborate wigs with decorated headbands. Wigs were often made into long plaits or tresses. The wigs were often made of human hair, but sometimes sheep's wool was used. Poorer women sold their hair to the wig makers.

Many men in ancient Egypt also shaved their heads and wore wigs. They shaved their faces to keep cool and clean. No one had a mustache. A beard was a sign of authority or wisdom, and rulers wore a false beard at feasts or festivals. On these occasions women wore lotus flowers in their hair. Both men and women wore ointments and perfumes.

Scented wax

Guests at banquets sometimes placed a cake or ball of scented wax on their heads. During the heat of a long evening, the wax melted and gave off a sweet scent.

◄ These musicians are playing at a banquet. You can see the cones of wax on their heads.

FESTIVALS AND FUN

The ancient Egyptians held festivals at different times of the year. Most festivals were held in honor of their many gods and goddesses. Ordinary people were given holidays so that they could take part in the processions and celebrations at the temple that was the "home" of a particular god or goddess. Some texts from the Middle and New Kingdoms told people to enjoy themselves throughout their lives. One says: "... cease not to drink, to eat.... Have holidays and do what you please every day and night."

Getting ready for a feast

People in ancient Egypt loved parties. They sometimes held feasts that lasted all day. They invited special guests, and all wore their best clothes. Men and women wore jewelry and makeup.

Imagine that you are going to an Egyptian feast. You will wear a jeweled collar and paint your face so that you will look your best.

Paint your face like an ancient Egyptian

You will need: • black and red face paints, or black eyeliner and red lipstick • a mirror.

1. Close one eye. Remember to keep it closed until the paint dries. Starting next to your nose, paint a thick black line along your eyelid, just above your eyelashes. Continue the line about half an inch beyond your eye.

2. Paint another line above the first one.

3. Paint a thick black line along your eyebrow. Take it as far as the other lines. Let the paint dry.

4. Do the same for the other eye.

5. Use the paint or lipstick to color your lips red.

Make a decorated collar

You will need: • a pencil • a ruler • some thick paper about 16 x 12 in. (40 x 30 cm) • a pair of scissors • paints or coloring pencils • 2 safety pins.

1. Place the paper with the long edges at the top and bottom. Fold it in half, from left to right.

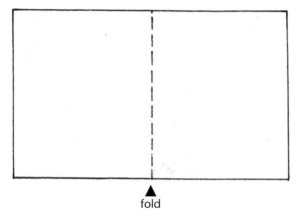

fold

2. Measure 5 in. (13 cm) along the top left-hand edge. Mark the point with your pencil. Now mark 3 in. (7.6 cm) down the left-hand side. Draw a curved line between these points. Draw a curved line from the top right-hand corner to the bottom left-hand corner. Cut along these curved lines.

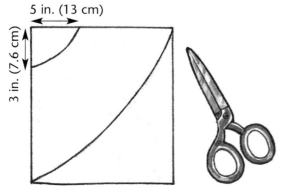

5 in. (13 cm)

3 in. (7.6 cm)

3. Open out the paper. Make four pencil marks along the top of each side of your collar, to divide it into five. Draw a curved line from one side to the other, between each pair of marks.

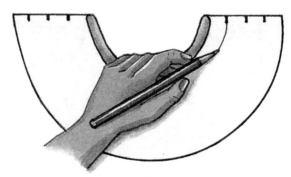

4. Decorate your collar using paints or pencils. You could copy the one in the picture or use some of the other patterns that you can see in the photographs earlier in this book.

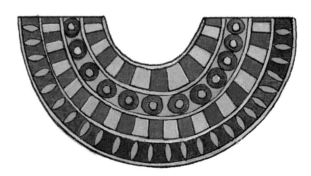

5. When the collar is ready, pin it to your clothes at the shoulders with the two safety pins.

The snake game

Children in ancient Egypt loved toys and games. Toy animals were very popular, especially horses on wheels, which children could pull or push along. Craft workers usually made toys out of wood or clay.

Children played the snake game on a stone board or plate. The children used sticks that had one curved side and one flat side. They threw the sticks into the air, and then counted how many landed with the flat side up. There were no dice in ancient Egypt. Make a snakeboard and play this game.

You will need: • a piece of thick paper about 8 x 12 in. (20 x 30 cm) • a pencil • a black felt-tipped pen • some coloring pens, paints, or pencils • a pair of scissors • Popsicle sticks.

1.   Draw a big snake on the paper, like the one in the picture. Draw four small circles–these will be your playing pieces.

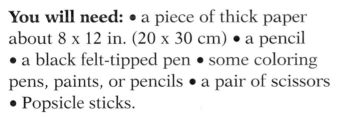

2.   Paint the snake yellow and the jewels on its neck red, blue, and green. Paint each playing piece a different color. When the paint is dry, use the black felt-tipped pen to

mark out the playing squares on the snake's body. Paint some of the squares red.

3.   Cut out the snake and the playing pieces.

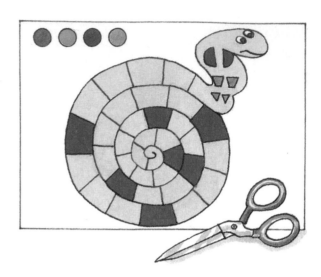

4.   Draw or paint a red snake on one side of each of the popsicle sticks. These will be your throwing sticks. Now you are ready to play your game.

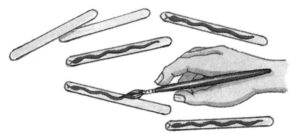

5.   Up to four people can play, or you could play on your own by racing two playing pieces against each other. Start each playing piece on the snake's head. Take turns to throw the six sticks into the air. When they land, count the number of sticks that show the snake. That is the number of squares you can move your playing piece along the snake. Beware! If you land on a red square, you must go back to the beginning. The winner is the first player who reaches the snake's tail.

Make an Egyptian pot

Egyptian craft workers made pots and bowls from clay, stone, and glass. People used pots at home and at work. The best pieces were kept for special occasions. You can make an Egyptian pot to hold your favorite things.

You will need • some clay (the kind that dries hard) • paints and a brush • a Popsicle stick or a blunt knife.

1. Look at the pictures of pots and choose which type of pot to make.

2. Break off lumps from your clay and roll the lumps into ropes.

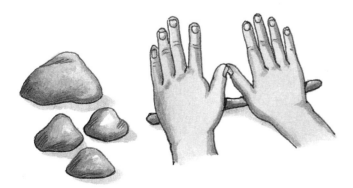

3. Coil a rope around to make a base for your pot. Now coil more ropes to build up the shape of the pot. Make the clay stick by wetting it with a little water or by pressing the joints together.

4. Use your stick or knife to smooth the surface of the pot. Let it dry.

5. When the clay is hard, you can paint it. Choose a reddish-orange, turquoise blue, black, white, and yellow. Some Egyptian pots are all one color. Others have patterns like the ones in the picture.

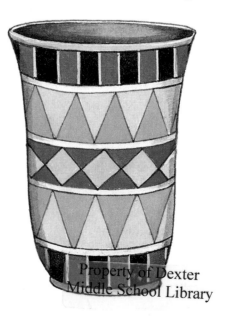

GLOSSARY

adz: A sharp cutting tool for shaping wood or stone.

alabaster: A whitish translucent mineral often carved into figures and vases.

amulet: A decoration made of stone, wood, or glass, worn to protect the wearer against evil.

archaeologist: Someone who studies the past by digging up or examining ancient ruins, remains, and writings.

charcoal: Pieces of burned, blackened wood, used for drawing or for making ink.

cobalt: A grey metal that is used to make blue coloring for pottery glazes or glass.

craft: Any trade or pastime in which people use skill to make things by hand.

enamel: A glassy coating applied to metal or other surfaces and then fired or baked to harden it.

faience: A thick paste made from sand or quartz mixed with lime, and colored blue or green, commonly used to make small figures of animals and people.

fibers: Strong, thread-like parts of a plant.

flax: A plant whose tough, stringy stems are used to make linen.

geometric: Made up of repeated lines and angles, such as zigzags.

gypsum: A mineral of calcium and sulphur. Alabaster is a kind of gypsum.

henna: Plant that produces a red dye, used to color hair and cloth.

hieroglyph: The script used by ancient Egyptians. It was made up of many tiny pictures or symbols. These symbols represent words and sounds.

inlaid: Decorated with a design that is set into a surface. The surface is carved out so that the decoration fits into it exactly and is level with it.

kiln: An oven that can heat material such as clay to a very high temperature.

lapis-lazuli: A blue semi-precious stone.

loincloth: A piece of cloth wrapped around the waist, sometimes hanging like a very short skirt, or passed between the legs, like a pair of shorts.

loom: A wooden frame for weaving thread into cloth.

malachite: A green mineral of copper that can be easily polished to a shine. Azurite, a blue mineral also of copper, usually is found with malachite.

molding: To work something into a particular shape by hand, or to pour or press it into a hollow form, called a mold.

mummy: A dead body that was preserved with ointments. The body was wrapped tightly with strips of cloth.

obelisk: A tall, four-sided pillar, shaped like a pyramid at the top.

papyrus: A reed that grows in the Nile River. The reeds were peeled and cut into strips. The strips were soaked in water to make them soft, then placed across one another, pressed, and dried to form a writing material.

parchment: Paper made from the skin of animals, usually sheep or goats.

preserve: To stop from decaying, or going bad.

pyramids: The stone burial places of pharaohs and rich nobles. The four sloping sides stood on a square base. The sides met at a point at the top.

quartz: A mineral that has many different forms, including some gemstones. Quartz sometimes contains precious metals.

senet: A popular Egyptian board game that was played like backgammon.

silt: The fine mud that is left behind by river floods. Egyptians used it for making bricks.

smelting: Heating metal to shape it into weapons, tools, or decorations.

FURTHER READING

Ancient Egypt. Art and Civilization (series). Marco Nardi and John Malam (NTC/Contemporary Publishing Company)

Ancient Egypt. History Beneath Your Feet (series). Jane Shuter (Raintree/Steck-Vaughn)

Ancient Egypt. My World (series). Amanda Martin and Kate Hayden (World Book, Inc.)

The Ancient Egyptians. Understanding People of the Past (series). Rosemary Rees (Heinemann)

Ancient Egyptians and Their Neighbors: An Activity Guide. Marian Broida (Chicago Review Press)

Egypt. Countries of the World (series). Susan L. Wilson (Gareth Stevens)

The Egyptian News. The History News (series). Scott Steedman (Gareth Stevens)

The Egyptians. Crafts from the Past (series). Gillian Chapman (Heinemann)

The Egyptians. People of the Past (series). Denise Allard (Gareth Stevens)

Technology in the Time of Ancient Egypt. Technology in the Time Of (series). Judith Crosher (Raintree/Steck-Vaughn)

INDEX